Five Minutes to Reading Music:

A Road Map to Musical Success

INCLUDES REPRODUCIBLE LESSONS!
3-5 MINUTES A DAY TO READING MUSIC

by Jerry Estes

Shawnee Press

EXCLUSIVELY DISTRIBUTED BY

7777 W. BLUEMOUND RD. P.O. BOX 13819 MILWAUKEE, WI 53213

Visit Shawnee Press Online at www.shawneepress.com

ISBN 978-1-59235-114-5

Copyright © 2007, Shawnee Press, Inc., Nashville, TN 37212
International Copyright Secured   All Rights Reserved

The publisher hereby grants permission for pages 6-47 of this book to be reproduced for classroom use. This is a nontransferable license.

Table of Contents

To the Director 3
Starting Pitches Overview 4-5
Introduction 6
Road Trip One 7-14
    Road Trip One End 15
    Activity #1 16
    Activity #2 17
About Road Trip Two 18
    Road Trip Two 19-26
    Road Trip Two End 27
    Activity #1 28
About Road Trip Three 29
    Road Trip Three 30-37
    Road Trip Three End 38
About Road Trip Four 39
    Road Trip Four 40-47
You Did It! 48

To the Director...

Welcome to "Five Minutes to Reading Music: A Road Map to Musical Success!" This series of short exercises is designed to address two problems facing most choral directors today. First, students who enroll in your chorus often arrive with little or no sight-reading skills. Second, the limited amount of rehearsals does not provide adequate time for accomplishing all you would like to do. My experience in over 25 years of teaching is that most choral sight-reading series work well at the beginning of the year, but as concerts approach they get used less and less, resulting in music being taught "by rote," with singers continuing to lack this very important skill.

These reproducible exercises are easy to use and should take no more than 3 to 5 minutes at the beginning of each rehearsal. When first introducing them to your chorus, give each singer a copy of pages six and seven, which explain the concept and start the process with miles 1 through 5. Each week after that, distribute one page to each singer. Feel free to use them in different ways; for example, experienced choruses could sing an entire page without stopping, using the exercises as a review, or if your chorus is really inexperienced, you may want to try repeating a page for a second week. Another suggestion would be to use the exercises as "bookends" for your rehearsals; have them sing that day's exercise at the beginning, then have them perform the same one just before packing up.

Starting pitches for all exercises can be found on pages 4 and 5.

Here are some important features:

- This series can be used with mixed or treble choruses.
- It covers an entire school year, based upon 8 weeks per quarter (allowing for inevitable missed days).
- Road Trips One and Two emphasize melodic elements with no variance in rhythms.
- Road Trips Three and Four include the addition of exercises written in contrapuntal style, more advanced rhythmic patterns, minor keys, and 3/4 time signature. Also included in these two trips is a feature called "Rhythm for the Road." These 4-measure patterns are designed to function as accompaniments for each of the 5 melodic exercises while providing a variety of opportunities for study of rhythmic values. It is suggested that a small group of students be chosen to play the accompaniment on a rotating basis.
- Road Trips One and Two are arranged in 2-part mixed voicing. (Treble Choruses should sing only the upper part, in unison.)
- Road Trips Three and Four are arranged in 3-part mixed voicing. (Treble Choruses should sing the two upper parts.)
- The Baritone part never exceeds a range of a 5th.

- Any time the Gas Station Attendant is pictured at the bottom of a page, it is time for a checkup to assess the understanding of material recently covered. The 5th exercise on each page was intentionally left unlabeled giving your students a chance to challenge themselves to correctly identify the appropriate solfege symbols.
- In Road Trips Three and Four, the exercises are all placed on staves. As before, every 5th pattern is left unlabeled.
- Included throughout the series are "Travel Tips" (thoughts regarding vocal health, being a good chorus member, etc.) and "Points of Interest" (giving attention to elements covered, such as perfect 4ths, stepwise movement, etc.)
- At the end of Trips One, Two and Three, there are suggested activities which are related to the material previously covered. These activities are designed to be helpful in meeting some state and national fine arts standards.

Remember, these exercises are intended to take only 3 to 5 minutes of rehearsal time...so if you find yourself spending more time than that, stop! The secret to success is to consistently use them daily for a short time.

Best of luck!
Jerry Estes

Overview of Material Covered

Road Trip One

| Do=C | $\dfrac{D\ ^R}{D\ _S}$ | ♩ 𝄽 |

| Do=C | $\dfrac{D\ ^R}{D\ _S}$ | ♩ 𝄽 (same as above, on staff) |

| Do=C | $\dfrac{D\ R\ ^M}{D\ _L\ _S}$ | ♩ 𝄽 |

| Do=C | $\dfrac{D\ R\ ^M}{D\ _L\ _S}$ | ♩ 𝄽 (same as above, on staff) |

| Do=C | $\dfrac{D\ R\ ^{M\ S}}{D\ ^T\ _L\ _S}$ | ♩ 𝄽 |

| Do=C | $\dfrac{D\ R\ ^{M\ S}}{D\ ^T\ _L\ _S}$ | ♩ 𝄽 (same as above, on staff) |

| Do=C | $\dfrac{D\ R\ ^{M\ F\ S}}{D\ ^R\ ^T\ _L\ _S}$ | ♩ 𝄽 |

| Do=C | $\dfrac{D\ R\ ^{M\ F\ S}}{D\ ^R\ ^T\ _L\ _S}$ | ♩ 𝄽 (same as above, on staff) |

Road Trip Two

| Do=G | $\dfrac{D\ ^S}{D\ ^R}$ | ♩ 𝄽 |

| Do=G | $\dfrac{D\ ^S}{D\ ^R}$ | ♩ 𝄽 (same as above, on staff) |

| Do=G | $\dfrac{D\ _L\ ^S}{D\ R\ ^M}$ | ♩ 𝄽 |

| Do=G | $\dfrac{D\ _L\ ^S}{D\ R\ ^M}$ | ♩ 𝄽 (same as above, on staff) |

| Do=G | $\dfrac{D\ ^T\ _L\ ^S}{D\ R\ ^{M\ S}}$ | ♩ 𝄽 |

| Do=G | $\dfrac{D\ ^T\ _L\ ^S}{D\ R\ ^{M\ S}}$ | ♩ 𝄽 (same as above, on staff) |

| Do=G | $\dfrac{D\ ^R\ ^T\ _L\ ^S}{D\ R\ ^{M\ F\ S}}$ | ♩ 𝄽 |

| Do=G | $\dfrac{D\ ^R\ ^T\ _L\ ^S}{D\ R\ ^{M\ F\ S}}$ | ♩ 𝄽 (same as above, on staff) |

Overview of Material Covered

Road Trip Three

| Do=C | $\dfrac{D\ R\ ^{M\ S}}{D\ _{L\ S}}$ | ♩ 𝄾 (new patterns) |

| Do=G | $\dfrac{D\ _{L\ S}}{D\ R\ ^{M\ S}}$ | (same patterns as above) |

| Do=C | $\dfrac{D\ R\ ^{M\ S}}{D\ _{L\ S}}$ | ♩ 𝄾 ♩ – |

| Do=G | $\dfrac{D\ _{L\ S}}{D\ R\ ^{M\ S}}$ | (same patterns as above) |

| Do=C | $\dfrac{D\ R\ ^{M\ F\ S}}{D\ _{T\ L\ S}}$ | ♩ 𝄾 ♩ – ♫ |

| Do=G | $\dfrac{D\ _{T\ L\ S}}{D\ R\ ^{M\ F\ S}}$ | (same patterns as above) |

| Do=C | $\dfrac{D\ R\ ^{M\ F\ S}}{D\ ^{R}\ _{T\ L\ S}}$ | ♩ 𝄾 ♩ – ♫ 𝅝 |

| Do=G | $\dfrac{D\ ^{R}\ _{T\ L\ S}}{D\ R\ ^{M\ F\ S}}$ | (same patterns as above) |

Road Trip Four

| Do=C | $\dfrac{D\ R\ ^{M\ F\ S}}{D\ ^{R}\ _{T\ L\ S}}$ | ♩ 𝄾 ♩ – ♫ |

| Do=G | $\dfrac{D\ ^{R}\ _{T\ L\ S}}{D\ R\ ^{M\ F\ S}}$ | (same patterns as above) |

| Do=C | $\dfrac{D\ R\ ^{M\ F\ S}}{D\ ^{R}\ _{T\ L\ S}}$ | ♩ 𝄾 ♩ – ♫ ♬♩ |

| Do=G | $\dfrac{D\ ^{R}\ _{T\ L\ S}}{D\ R\ ^{M\ F\ S}}$ | (same patterns as above) |

| Do=E♭ | $\dfrac{_{L\ T}\ D\ R\ ^{M}}{_{L\ S\ M}}$ | (same patterns as above) |

| Do=B♭ | $\dfrac{_{L}\ S\ ^{M}}{_{L\ T}\ D\ R\ ^{M}}$ | (same patterns as above) |

| Do=E♭ | $\dfrac{_{L\ T}\ D\ R\ ^{M}}{_{M}\ ^{F\ S\ L}}$ | (same patterns as above) |

| Do=B♭ | $\dfrac{_{R}\ ^{M\ F\ S\ L}}{_{L\ T}\ D\ R\ ^{M}}$ | |

— relative minor — contrapuntal —

Five Minutes to Reading Music:
A Road Map to Musical Success

Welcome to "Five Minutes to Reading Music: A Road Map to Musical Success!" You are about to begin the first section of a journey, one especially designed with you in mind. When all four sections of this journey are completed, you will know a lot more about reading choral music. Each exercise should take 3 or 5 minutes at the beginning of the rehearsal. It is not important that you "learn" each one . . . the goal is for you to train your eyes, ears, brain and singing voice to work together.

The syllables you will sing are based upon a method of learning called "The Solfege Method." You might have already used this method in other music classes, and your teacher may want to explain in more detail, but for now you only need to know how to pronounce the following syllables:

Do (doh)

Ti (tee)

La (lah)

Sol (soh)

To sing a scale
start here . . . then continue upwards

Fa (fah)

Mi (mee)

Re (reh)

Do (doh)

You should remember that the syllables always keep their relationship to each other the same. For example, "Do" up to "Sol" is always a distance of five scale steps.

For now the emphasis will be upon where the notes are placed in the music, and practicing singing what is shown on the page. For this reason the rhythms, or how long each note or rest lasts, have been kept very simple. In later sections we will practice a wider variety of rhythmic patterns, including notes and rests.

Finally, please make an effort to do your very best when singing these short exercises, paying close attention to the **travel tips** and **points of interest** included on each page. Bon voyage!

Copyright © 2007, Shawnee Press, Inc., Nashville, TN 37212

Road Trip One

	D D D 𝄽	R R R 𝄽	D D R R	D 𝄽 𝄽 𝄽
upper voices				
lower voices				
	D D D 𝄽		D D	D 𝄽 𝄽 𝄽
		S S S 𝄽	S S	

	D D D 𝄽	D R R 𝄽	D D R R	D 𝄽 𝄽 𝄽
upper voices				
lower voices				
	D D D 𝄽	D	D D	D 𝄽 𝄽 𝄽
		S S 𝄽	S S	

Travel Tip

Always hear the notes in your head before you open your mouth to sing!

	D R D 𝄽	D R D 𝄽	D R D R	D 𝄽 𝄽 𝄽
upper voices				
lower voices				
	D D 𝄽	D D 𝄽	D D	D 𝄽 𝄽 𝄽
	S	S	S S	

	D D R 𝄽	R R D 𝄽	R R D R	D 𝄽 𝄽 𝄽
upper voices				
lower voices				
	D D	D 𝄽	D	D 𝄽 𝄽 𝄽
	S 𝄽	S S	S S S	

	D R R 𝄽	R D D 𝄽	D R D R	D 𝄽 𝄽 𝄽
upper voices				
lower voices				
	D	D D 𝄽	D D	D 𝄽 𝄽 𝄽
	S S 𝄽	S	S S	

Copyright © 2007, Shawnee Press, Inc., Nashville, TN 37212

Road Trip One

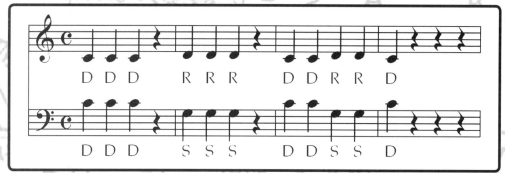

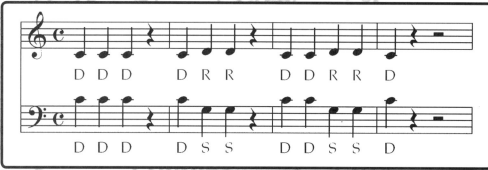

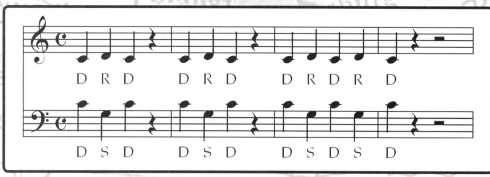

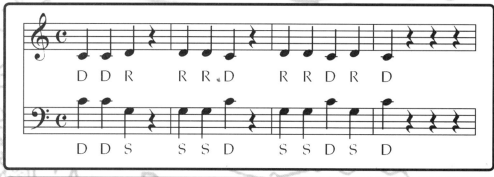

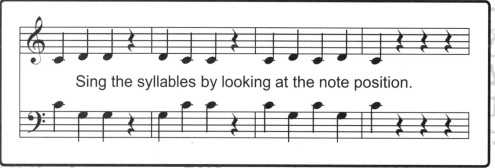

Sing the syllables by looking at the note position.

Point of Interest

Note that there are no skips in the melodies of this week's exercises. They all either stay the same or move stepwise.

TIME FOR A 10 MILE CHECK-UP!

Copyright © 2007, Shawnee Press, Inc., Nashville, TN 37212

Road Trip One

MILE 11

D D D 𝄽	R R R 𝄽	M M R R	D 𝄽 𝄽 𝄽
upper voices			
lower voices			
D D D 𝄽	S S S 𝄽	L L S S	D 𝄽 𝄽 𝄽

MILE 12

D D R 𝄽	M M R 𝄽	D D R R	D 𝄽 𝄽 𝄽
upper voices			
lower voices			
D D S 𝄽	L L L 𝄽	L L S S	D 𝄽 𝄽 𝄽

MILE 13

D R M 𝄽	M R D 𝄽	D R M	D 𝄽 𝄽 𝄽
upper voices			
lower voices			
D L S 𝄽	S L D 𝄽	D L S L	D 𝄽 𝄽 𝄽

MILE 14

D R R 𝄽	M R R 𝄽	M M R R	D 𝄽 𝄽 𝄽
upper voices			
lower voices			
D S S 𝄽	S L L 𝄽	D D S S	D 𝄽 𝄽 𝄽

MILE 15

D R D 𝄽	M R M 𝄽	D R M M	D 𝄽 𝄽 𝄽
upper voices			
lower voices			
D L S 𝄽	D L D 𝄽	D L S S	D 𝄽 𝄽 𝄽

Travel Tip

Remember to sing these exercises with a relaxed jaw, lifted soft palate and flattened tongue. Always practice good choral singing!

Copyright © 2007, Shawnee Press, Inc., Nashville, TN 37212

Road Trip One

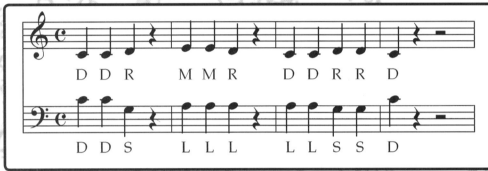
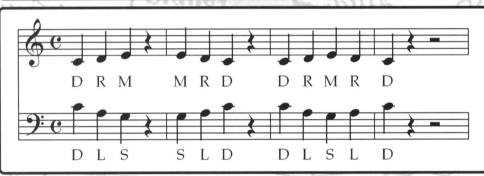
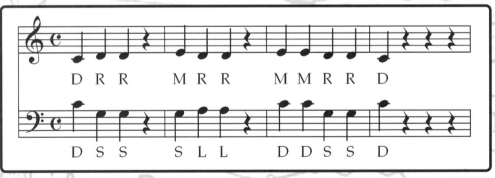
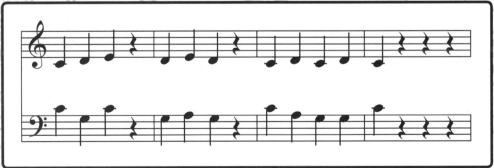

"Do" up to "Re" is called a Major 2nd (find it in the upper part) "Do" down to "Sol" is called a Perfect 4th (find it in the lower part)

TIME FOR A 20 MILE CHECK-UP!

Copyright © 2007, Shawnee Press, Inc., Nashville, TN 37212

Road Trip One

MILE 21

upper voices			
D R M ♪	M S S ♪	M M R R	D ♪ ♪ ♪

lower voices			
D T D ♪	D T T ♪	D D T T	D ♪ ♪ ♪

MILE 22

upper voices			
D R M ♪	M S M ♪	M S M R	D ♪ ♪ ♪

lower voices			
D T D ♪	L T D ♪	L T S S	D ♪ ♪ ♪

MILE 23

upper voices			
D M S ♪	S M D ♪	D M S M	D ♪ ♪ ♪

lower voices			
D S D ♪	T T D ♪	S S T T	D ♪ ♪ ♪

MILE 24

upper voices			
D M S ♪	M R M ♪	S M R R	D ♪ ♪ ♪

lower voices			
D L S ♪	T T D ♪	D S L T	D ♪ ♪ ♪

MILE 25

upper voices			
D M M ♪	R M M ♪	S M D R	D ♪ ♪ ♪

lower voices			
D S S ♪	T D D ♪	S L S T	D ♪ ♪ ♪

Travel Tip

A choir is similar to an athletic team. The members can only contribute 100% if they are healthy and well-rested.

Copyright © 2007, Shawnee Press, Inc., Nashville, TN 37212

Road Trip One

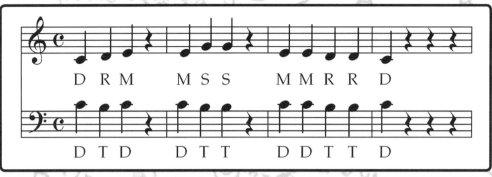
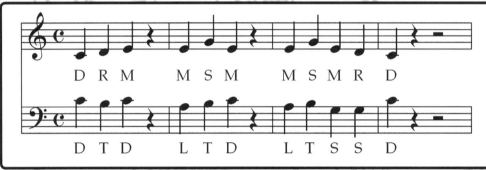

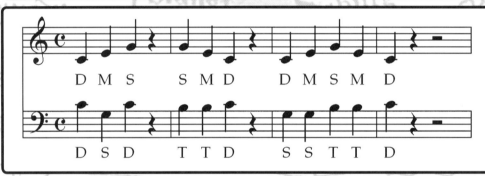

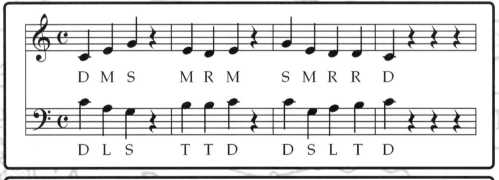

Point of Interest

Have everyone in the group choose one pitch from Mile 28, upper part, and sing at the same time. It sounds good because all pitches are taken from something called the Tonic Chord

TIME FOR A 30 MILE CHECK-UP!

Copyright © 2007, Shawnee Press, Inc., Nashville, TN 37212

Road Trip One

MILE 31

D R M 𝄽	M F S 𝄽	S F M R	D 𝄽 𝄽 𝄽
upper voices			
lower voices			
D R D 𝄽	D T D 𝄽	T T L T	D 𝄽 𝄽 𝄽

MILE 32

D R M 𝄽	M F M 𝄽	M F M R	D 𝄽 𝄽 𝄽
upper voices			
lower voices			
D T D 𝄽	D R D 𝄽	S L S T	D 𝄽 𝄽 𝄽

MILE 33

D M S 𝄽	S F F 𝄽	M M F M	D 𝄽 𝄽 𝄽
upper voices			
lower voices			
D D S 𝄽	T L L 𝄽	S S T T	D 𝄽 𝄽 𝄽

MILE 34

D M S 𝄽	M R M 𝄽	S M R R	D 𝄽 𝄽 𝄽
upper voices			
lower voices			
D T D 𝄽	T L S 𝄽	L L T T	D 𝄽 𝄽 𝄽

MILE 35

D M S 𝄽	F F M 𝄽	S F M R	D 𝄽 𝄽 𝄽
upper voices			
lower voices			
D D T 𝄽	L T D 𝄽	D R D T	D 𝄽 𝄽 𝄽

Travel Tip

Breath management means that you utilize proper breathing as related to singing. Try performing the exercises very slowly, and remember to apply breath management as you do so.

Road Trip One

MILE 36
D R M   M F S   S F M R D
D R D   D T D   T T L T D

MILE 37
D R M   M F M   M F M R D
D T D   D R D   S L S T D

MILE 38
D M S   S F F   M M F M D
D S D   T L L   S S T T D

MILE 39
D M S   M R M   S M R R D
D T D   T L S   L L T T D

MILE 40

Point of Interest

A unison is when two or more sections of a group perform the same pitch. Look for places where the upper and lower parts sing in unison.

TIME FOR A 40 MILE CHECK-UP!

Copyright © 2007, Shawnee Press, Inc., Nashville, TN 37212

Time to stop for the night!

Congratulations! You just completed the first section of our journey. In this section you concentrated mainly on singing notes ("Do" up to "Sol" for the upper voices, and "Do" down to "Sol" for the lower voices). In the next section the pitches will be switched, with the upper voices singing the same patterns the lower voices did, and vice versa.

Before you continue on with Road Trip Two, please take a little break and do the following activities:

1. **Composition:** Using any combination of pitches and rhythms taken from Miles 1-40, write your own composition. It would be best if you use pitches from your own voice part (upper or lower) if applicable. Remember to give each measure 4 beats, and make your composition 4 measures in length.

When you are finished, you may want to perform it for the class. One idea would be to choose helpers—some to play the rhythms on percussion instruments as accompaniment, and others to sing the pitches with you.
See page 16 for the activity page.

2. **Notation:** Using a piano with the keys marked or some type of tone blocks, one volunteer should improvise a melody using tones and rhythms from Miles 1-40. The rest of the class must try and write down what is played.
See page 17 for the activity page.

3. **Improvisation:** Form a group of several students, each one with a percussion instrument. Spend a few minutes playing together with everybody making up their own rhythm. Use combinations of quarter notes, quarter rests, and eighth notes. (Eighth notes are sounded by playing 2 equal notes per beat, twice as many as a quarter note. These will be included in future Road Trips.)

When the group is ready, perform their rhythms as an accompaniment while the rest of the class sings one of the exercises from Miles 1-40.
No activity page necessary for this exercise.

Activity #1: Composition

NAME:

In the space below, using any combination of pitches and rhythms taken from Miles 1-40, write your own composition. It would be best if you use pitches from your own voice part (upper or lower) if applicable. Remember to give each measure 4 beats, and make your composition 4 measures in length. There are 3 spaces provided so that you can experiment with different ideas if you'd like.

When you are finished, you may want to perform it for the class. One idea would be to choose helpers, some to play the rhythms on percussion instruments as accompaniment, and others to sing the pitches with you.

Measure 1	Measure 2	Measure 3	Measure 4

Measure 1	Measure 2	Measure 3	Measure 4

Measure 1	Measure 2	Measure 3	Measure 4

Copyright © 2007, Shawnee Press, Inc., Nashville, TN 37212

Activity #2: Notation

NAME: _____

One volunteer should improvise a 4-measure melody and sing it, using any combination of pitches and rhythms taken from Miles 1-40. It would be best to use pitches from his/her own voice part (upper or lower) if applicable. As in Activity #1, each measure should have 4 beats.

The rest of the group must try and notate (write down) the notes and rhythms they hear, using the blank spaces provided below. Writing notes is not necessary; just write letters, but you will need to write a quarter rest each time it is performed.

Measure 1	Measure 2	Measure 3	Measure 4

Measure 1	Measure 2	Measure 3	Measure 4

Measure 1	Measure 2	Measure 3	Measure 4

About Road Trip Two...

Welcome to Road Trip Two! In this phase of our journey you will explore the other part of the "Do" to "Do" scale. It was divided this way because many singing voices cannot easily reach all 8 notes of the complete scale. Therefore, the pitch of "Do" has been changed to one that works better for most singers. The rhythms have been kept exactly the same so that you will be free to focus on the pitches of the notes in each melody. As a reminder, these exercises are based upon the singing method called "The Solfege Method." Below is a review of how to pronounce each one:

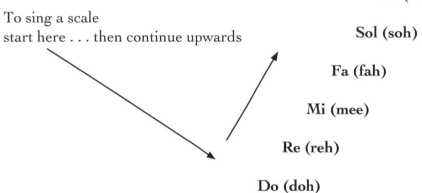

Once again, please make an effort to do your very best when singing these short exercises. Bon voyage!

Copyright © 2007, Shawnee Press, Inc., Nashville, TN 37212

Road Trip Two

| MILE 41 | D D D 𝄽
 upper voices S S S 𝄽
 lower voices

 D D D 𝄽   R R R 𝄽 | D D   S S

 D D R R | D 𝄽 𝄽 𝄽

 D 𝄽 𝄽 𝄽 |

| MILE 42 | D D D 𝄽   D   S S 𝄽
 upper voices
 lower voices

 D D D 𝄽   D R R 𝄽 | D D   S S

 D D R R | D 𝄽 𝄽 𝄽

 D 𝄽 𝄽 𝄽 |

| MILE 43 | D D 𝄽   D D 𝄽
 S   S
 upper voices
 lower voices

 D R D 𝄽   D R D 𝄽 | D   D
 S   S

 D R D R | D 𝄽 𝄽 𝄽

 D 𝄽 𝄽 𝄽 |

| MILE 44 | D D   D 𝄽
    S 𝄽 S S
 upper voices
 lower voices

 D D R 𝄽   R R D 𝄽 | D   D
 S   S

 R R   D R | D 𝄽 𝄽 𝄽

 D 𝄽 𝄽 𝄽 |

| MILE 45 | D   D D 𝄽
 S S 𝄽 S
 upper voices
 lower voices

 D R R 𝄽   R D D 𝄽 | D   D
   S   S

 D R D R | D 𝄽 𝄽 𝄽

 D 𝄽 𝄽 𝄽 |

Travel Tip

Drink lots of water... this will help keep your body tissues lubricated, including vocal cords.

Road Trip Two

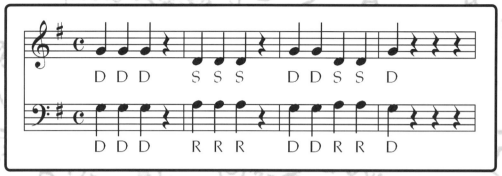

Point of Interest

Whenever the upper and lower voices both sing "Do" at the same time, they are singing what is called an octave, or two notes 8 steps apart.

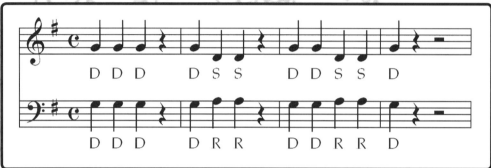

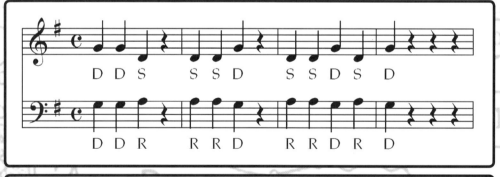

TIME FOR A 50 MILE CHECK-UP!

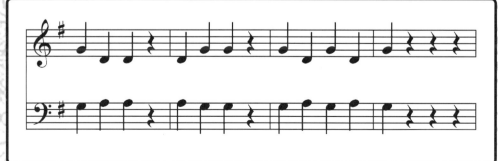

Copyright © 2007, Shawnee Press, Inc., Nashville, TN 37212

Road Trip Two

MILE 51

D D D 𝄽		L L S S	D 𝄽 𝄽 𝄽
	S S S 𝄽		
upper voices			
lower voices			
D D D 𝄽	R R R 𝄽	M M R R	D 𝄽 𝄽 𝄽

MILE 52

D D	L L L 𝄽	L L S S	D 𝄽 𝄽 𝄽
S 𝄽			
upper voices			
lower voices			
D D R 𝄽	M M R 𝄽	D D R R	D 𝄽 𝄽 𝄽

MILE 53

D L	S L D 𝄽	D L	D 𝄽 𝄽 𝄽
S 𝄽	S	S L	
upper voices			
lower voices			
D R M 𝄽	M R D 𝄽	D R M R	D 𝄽 𝄽 𝄽

MILE 54

D	S L L 𝄽	D D	D 𝄽 𝄽 𝄽
S S 𝄽		S S	
upper voices			
lower voices			
D R R 𝄽	M R R 𝄽	M M R R	D 𝄽 𝄽 𝄽

MILE 55

D	D D 𝄽	D	D 𝄽 𝄽 𝄽
L S 𝄽	L	L S S	
upper voices			
lower voices			
D R D 𝄽	M R M 𝄽	D R M M	D 𝄽 𝄽 𝄽

Travel Tip

To help eliminate nervousness before a performance, practice deep, controlled breathing. Inhale as slowly as possible through the nose four counts, hold seven counts, exhale through the mouth eight counts. Do at least twelve reps.

Road Trip Two

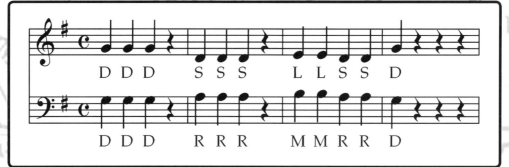

Point of Interest

Try and find the exercise in which the lower part is all stepwise movement (no skips or "stay the same").

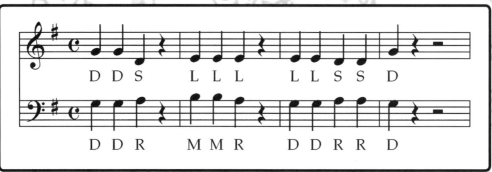

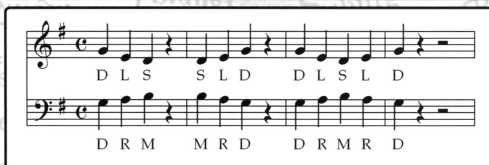

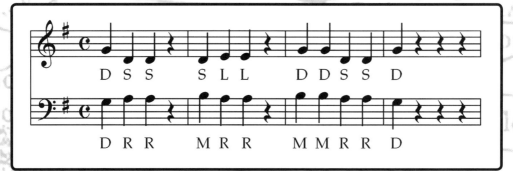

TIME FOR A 60 MILE CHECK-UP!

Copyright © 2007, Shawnee Press, Inc., Nashville, TN 37212

Road Trip Two

MILE 61

D T D 𝄽	D T T 𝄽	D D T T	D 𝄽 𝄽 𝄽

upper voices
lower voices

D R M 𝄽	M S S 𝄽	M M R R	D 𝄽 𝄽 𝄽

MILE 62

D T D 𝄽	L T D 𝄽	L T S S	D 𝄽 𝄽 𝄽

upper voices
lower voices

D R M 𝄽	M S M 𝄽	M S M R	D 𝄽 𝄽 𝄽

MILE 63

D S D 𝄽	T T D 𝄽	S S T T	D 𝄽 𝄽 𝄽

upper voices
lower voices

D M S 𝄽	S M D 𝄽	D M S M	D 𝄽 𝄽 𝄽

MILE 64

D L S 𝄽	T T D 𝄽	D S L T	D 𝄽 𝄽 𝄽

upper voices
lower voices

D M S 𝄽	M R M 𝄽	S M R R	D 𝄽 𝄽 𝄽

MILE 65

D S S 𝄽	T D D 𝄽	S L S T	D 𝄽 𝄽 𝄽

upper voices
lower voices

D M M 𝄽	R M M 𝄽	S M D R	D 𝄽 𝄽 𝄽

Travel Tip

Singing with a pleasant, lifted facial expression can help improve your intonation.

Copyright © 2007, Shawnee Press, Inc., Nashville, TN 37212

Road Trip Two

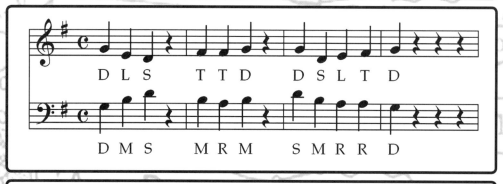

Point of Interest

Based upon what you learned in Road Trip One, try and find the exercise and voice part that contains the TONIC CHORD.

TIME FOR A 70 MILE CHECK-UP!

Road Trip Two

MILE 71

upper voices	D R D 𝄽	D T D 𝄽	T T L T	D 𝄽 𝄽 𝄽
lower voices	D R M 𝄽	M F S 𝄽	S F M R	D 𝄽 𝄽 𝄽

MILE 72

upper voices	D T D 𝄽	D R D 𝄽	S L S T	D 𝄽 𝄽 𝄽
lower voices	D R M 𝄽	M F M 𝄽	M F M R	D 𝄽 𝄽 𝄽

MILE 73

upper voices	D S D 𝄽	T L L 𝄽	S S T T	D 𝄽 𝄽 𝄽
lower voices	D M S 𝄽	S F F 𝄽	M M F M	D 𝄽 𝄽 𝄽

MILE 74

upper voices	D T D 𝄽	T L S 𝄽	L L T T	D 𝄽 𝄽 𝄽
lower voices	D M S 𝄽	M R M 𝄽	S M R R	D 𝄽 𝄽 𝄽

MILE 75

upper voices	D D T 𝄽	L T D 𝄽	D R D T	D 𝄽 𝄽 𝄽
lower voices	D M S 𝄽	F F M 𝄽	S F M R	D 𝄽 𝄽 𝄽

Travel Tip

Even when singing these exercises, try and make your voice sound expressive and beautiful.

Copyright © 2007, Shawnee Press, Inc., Nashville, TN 37212

Road Trip Two

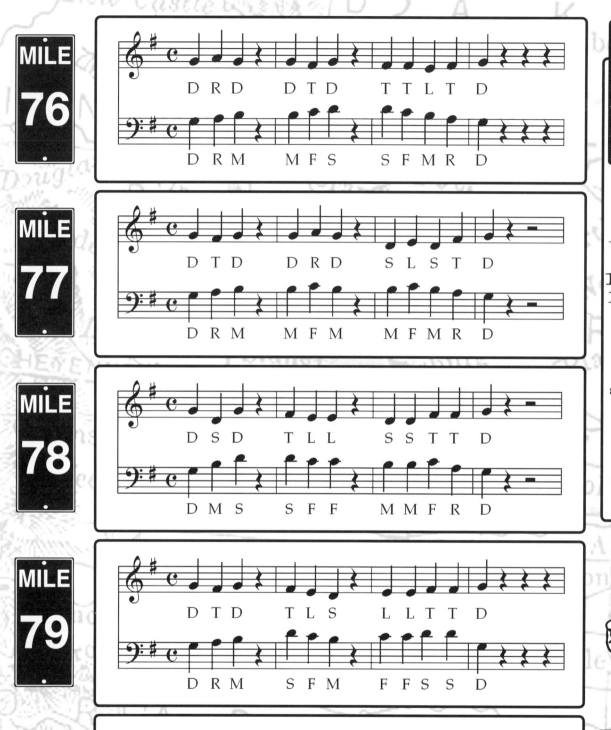

Point of Interest

The distance from "Sol" up to "Do" is called a PERFECT FOURTH. One easy way to remember what it sounds like is to sing the first four notes of "Here Comes the Bride."

TIME FOR AN 80 MILE CHECK-UP!

Copyright © 2007, Shawnee Press, Inc., Nashville, TN 37212

Time to stop for the night!

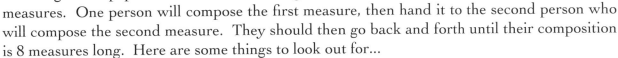

Another Road Trip completed! You are becoming a seasoned traveler, for sure. With 80 miles covered, you have explored the entire "Do" to "Do" scale. Road Trip Three will include a little more advanced part singing and also some rhythmic exercises, but you are a veteran... you can handle it!

Before you continue on with Road Trip Three, please take a little break and do the following activities:

1. **Composition:** This exercise will require you to think about how the melody should flow from one measure to the next. The class will need to divide into 2-person teams. Each team will be given a paper with boxes containing blank measures. One person will compose the first measure, then hand it to the second person who will compose the second measure. They should then go back and forth until their composition is 8 measures long. Here are some things to look out for...

- make sure the melody flows easily from measure to measure
- make sure it is easily singable
- try and give it a beginning, a middle, and an end (just like a good paragraph)
- make sure there are 4 beats in each measure

When all the teams have finished their compositions and practiced singing them, the class could have a concert with all the teams performing for each other.
See page 28 for the activity page.

2. **Constructive Criticism:** Another important skill for singers is to be able to listen to a performance and analyze it. After each team performs their composition from Activity #1, the rest of the group should offer comments and constructive criticism. The melodies should be analyzed using the criteria given in the directions above. It is VERY important, however, that all comments are carefully and thoughtfully spoken. In an activity such as this one, feeling safe is much more important than hearing hurtful comments, even though they may be true.
No activity page necessary for this exercise.

Copyright © 2007, Shawnee Press, Inc., Nashville, TN 37212

Activity #1: Composition

NAMES:

Divide the group into 2-person teams. Use the form below to write an 8 measure composition. Person #1 should write the first measure, then Person #2 should write the second measure. They keep passing it back and forth until they have completed 8 measures. It is important to make the melody flow from measure to measure, and also remember to have a beginning, a middle, and an end.

This time, instead of using only letters, write actual quarter notes and rests. You may want to refer to one of the previous pages for examples of how they should look.

Measure 1　　Measure 2　　Measure 3　　Measure 4

Measure 5　　Measure 6　　Measure 7　　Measure 8

About Road Trip Three...

Welcome to Road Trip Three! It will be a little different than the first two for several reasons. First, there are three voice parts instead of two. If your group is divided into Soprano (highest), Alto (middle), and Baritone (lowest), each section can find their melody line in the same arrangement-- top line (Soprano), middle line (Alto), and bottom line (Baritone). If your group has Tenor and Bass sections, they should both sing the bottom line.

Road Trip Three will also focus more on rhythms than the first two did. Each page of exercises will have a rhythm at the bottom. This rhythm is designed to work as an accompaniment for the five melody lines above it. There are many ways this can be done, but here are two suggestions . . .

• Before singing an exercise, the entire group can SAY or CLAP the rhythm. They can then divide into two groups, with one singing the numbered exercises and the other clapping the rhythmic accompaniment.

• A small group of students can clap or play the rhythm on various percussion instruments while the rest of the group sings. Each day a different group can perform the rhythmic accompaniment.

NOTE: There are several ways to teach rhythms, and each director will want to choose his/her preferred way. However, it is important to CLAP or PLAY the rhythms when accompanying the sung melodies; singing the rhythms would probably result in too much confusion.

Copyright © 2007, Shawnee Press, Inc., Nashville, TN 37212

Road Trip Three

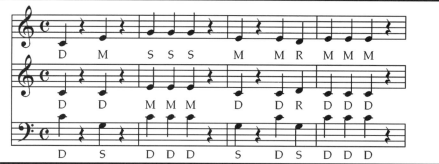

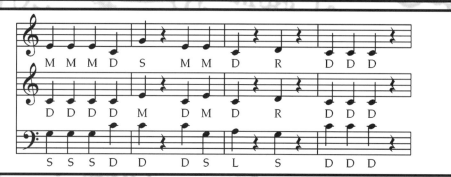

Travel Tip

If singing these exercises in 3 parts is difficult, try listening only to yourself and another person near you who is singing the same part. Always remember, however, that listening to the entire group is very important in most cases.

TIME FOR A 85 MILE CHECK-UP!

Rhythm for the Road: (Use with the exercises above)
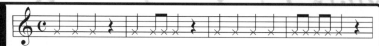

Copyright © 2007, Shawnee Press, Inc., Nashville, TN 37212

Road Trip Three

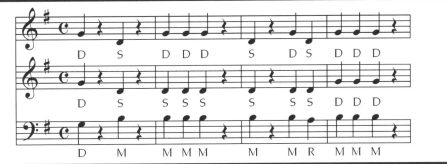

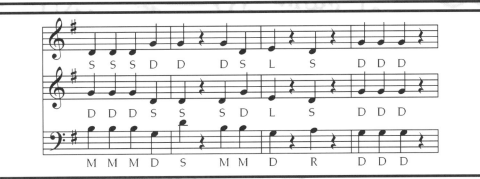

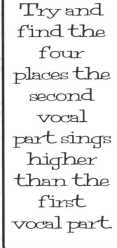

Point of Interest

Try and find the four places the second vocal part sings higher than the first vocal part.

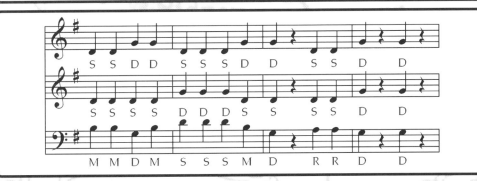

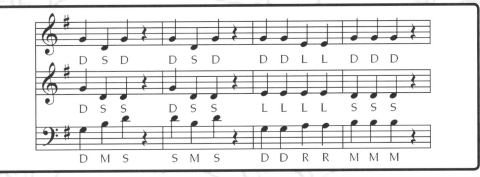

TIME FOR A 90 MILE CHECK-UP!

Rhythm for the Road:
(Use with the exercises above)

Copyright © 2007, Shawnee Press, Inc., Nashville, TN 37212

Road Trip Three

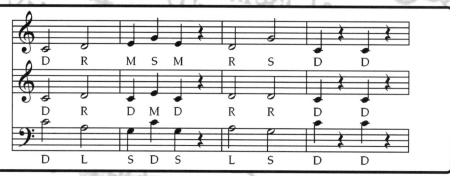

Travel Tip

When standing to sing, line up your frame (bones) properly, then let IT do the work while you relax and sing.

TIME FOR A 95 MILE CHECK-UP!

Rhythm for the Road: (Use with the exercises above)

Copyright © 2007, Shawnee Press, Inc., Nashville, TN 37212

Road Trip Three

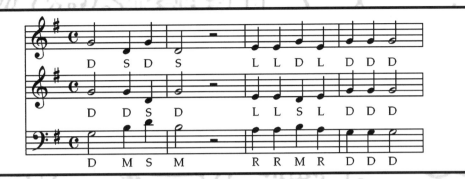

Point of Interest

Try and find the exercise which has absolutely no rests.

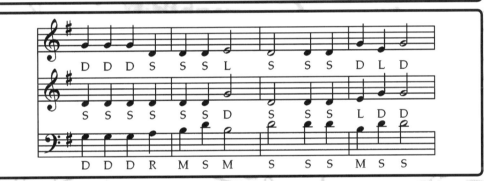

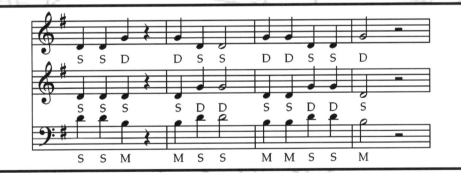

TIME FOR A 100 MILE CHECK-UP!

Road Trip Three

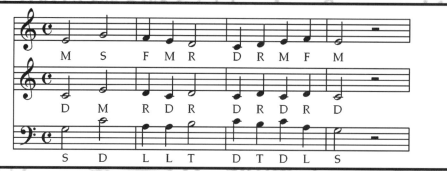

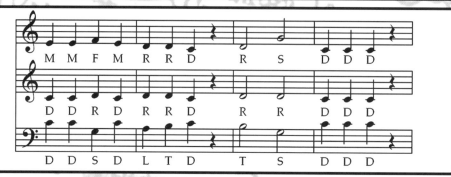

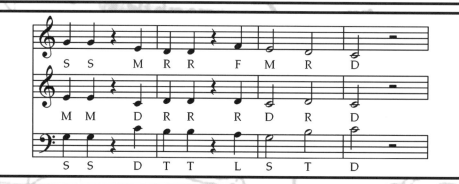

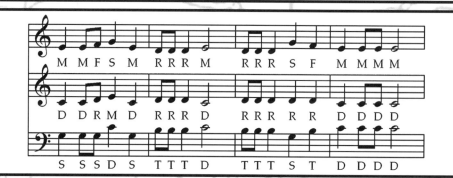

Road Trip Three

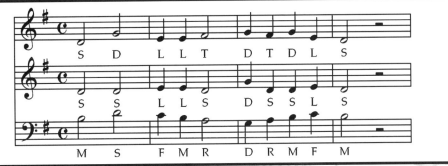

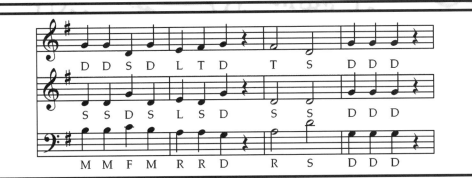

Point of Interest

The exercises for Mile 106 and Mile 108 end with a HALF REST (2 beats of silence).

TIME FOR A 110 MILE CHECK-UP!

Rhythm for the Road: (Use with the exercises above)

35

Copyright © 2007, Shawnee Press, Inc., Nashville, TN 37212

Road Trip Three

Travel Tip

Always try and analyze your part before it is time to sing. Don't be caught by surprise.

TIME FOR A 115 MILE CHECK-UP!

Rhythm for the Road: (Use with the exercises above)

Copyright © 2007, Shawnee Press, Inc., Nashville, TN 37212

Road Trip Three

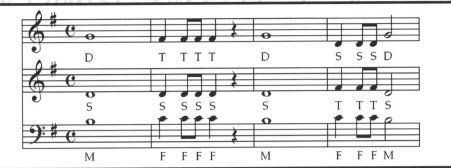

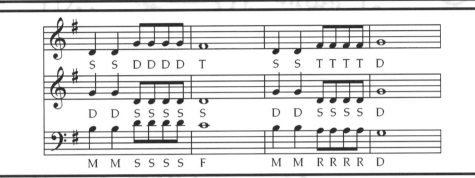

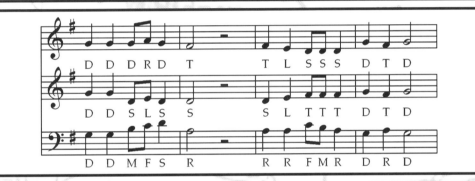

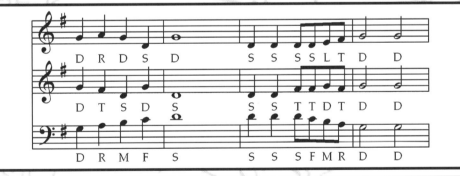

Point of Interest

Notice that the first note of all three parts for Mile 116 and Mile 118 make the sound of the TONIC CHORD. However, they are INVERTED, which means the position of the notes has been changed.

TIME FOR A 120 MILE CHECK-UP!

Rhythm for the Road: (Use with the exercises above)

Time to stop for the night!

Road Trip Three is complete . . . 120 miles under your belt! During this recent trip, you experienced many new sights, including singing more advanced harmonies and rhythms. You should feel much more confident in your ability to look at written music, know how it should sound, and sing it correctly the first time you try. This is called "sight-reading" in music, and it is a very valuable tool.

Before you continue on with Road Trip Four, please take a little break and do the following activities:

1. **Improvisation 1:** The following exercise may be a little challenging for some, but give it your best effort! Here is how it works . . .

- One student will sing a phrase using their own combination of notes from Miles 1-120
- The phrase should be 1 or 2 measures (4-8 beats) in length
- The class will then echo it
- The student leader should do at least 4 phrases
- The performance should have a beginning, a middle, and an end

If this exercise is a little difficult to understand, the director may want to demonstrate.
No activity page necessary for this exercise.

2. **Improvisation 2:** This exercise could be extremely challenging, but there are probably some students who are up to it! This takes two participants, and here is how it works . . .

- The first student CLAPS a rhythm, using any combination of notes (only quarter and eighth notes/rests should be used)
- The phrase should be 2 measures (8 beats) in length
- The second student then SINGS a phrase using any combination of note pitches/names, but must use the exact rhythms the first student has just performed.
- The two students should do at least 4 different patterns

No activity page necessary for this exercise.

Copyright © 2007, Shawnee Press, Inc., Nashville, TN 37212

About Road Trip Four...

Welcome to the final section of our journey! When you finish Road Trip Four, you will be able to say you are a seasoned traveler. Be prepared, however, because you are in for some challenges and adventures in the coming miles!

For example, many of the exercises are arranged in CONTRAPUNTAL style. This means that different voice parts are singing different rhythms at the same time. Road Trips One, Two and Three were all arranged in HOMOPHONIC style, with all the sections singing exactly the same rhythms and at the same time. When singing contrapuntal music, it may be a little harder to stay on your own part without being distracted by the others. It may be necessary for each section of the group to sing their part alone, then try adding one at a time until all three can sing together.

Another new adventure you will encounter on this Road Trip is that you will be singing in minor keys (the previous exercises were written in major keys). The main difference between major and minor keys is that minor keys create a different mood than major--a little more somber, or sad. They also usually end on "La," as opposed to "Do" for major keys.

Finally, you will also explore measures written in 3/4 time (Miles 156-160). This means that there are 3 beats per measure with a quarter note getting one beat. Up until now the exercises were made up of measures with 4 beats per measure. There are many other ways of dividing the beats in measures (called TIME SIGNATURES), but 4 beats per measure is the most common.

Good luck on this part of your journey!

Road Trip Four

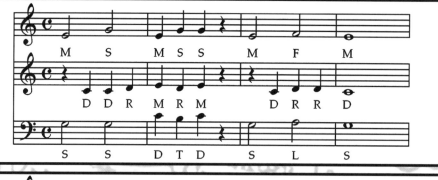

Travel Tip: If your part starts on a pitch different from "Do," find that pitch by starting on "Do" then singing up or down the scale until you reach it.

TIME FOR A 125 MILE CHECK-UP!

Rhythm for the Road: (Use with the exercises above)

Copyright © 2007, Shawnee Press, Inc., Nashville, TN 37212

Road Trip Four

Point of Interest

The melodies in these exercises are arranged in POLYPHONIC style, which means they do not all occur at the same time or have the same exact rhythms.

TIME FOR A 130 MILE CHECK-UP!

Rhythm for the Road
(Use with the exercises above)

Copyright © 2007, Shawnee Press, Inc., Nashville, TN 37212

Road Trip Four

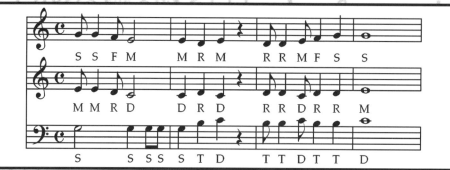

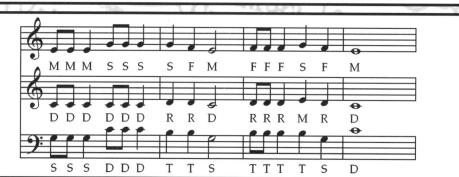

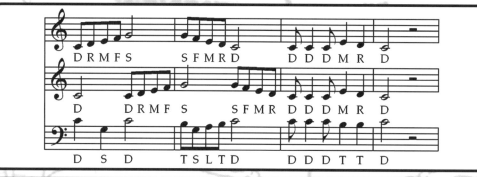

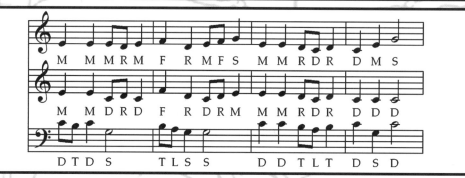

Road Trip Four

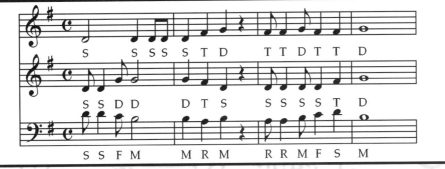

Point of Interest

Sometimes two notes in a chord can be right next to each other and still sound pleasant. Try and find an example in one of these exercises.

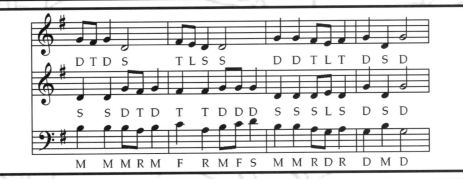

TIME FOR A 140 MILE CHECK-UP!

Rhythm for the Road:
(Use with the exercises above)

Copyright © 2007, Shawnee Press, Inc., Nashville, TN 37212

Road Trip Four

MILE 141

L D M D R T T L L D M D D L
L D D L T T T L L D D L L L
L S L L S S S L L S L L L L

Travel Tip

The less air you allow to flow through your vocal cords as you sing, the better you will sound

MILE 142

L L T T D D D D D R R M M M M M R D D T L
L L T T L L L L L T T D D D D T T L L T L
L S M M S L L L S S M M S L

MILE 143

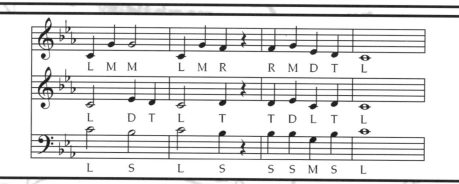

L M M L M R R M D T L
L D T L T T D L T L
L S L S S S M S L

MILE 144

L T D D R M R T D D R D T D
M L T T R L L T D R M
L M S S S L S L

TIME FOR A 145 MILE CHECK-UP!

MILE 145

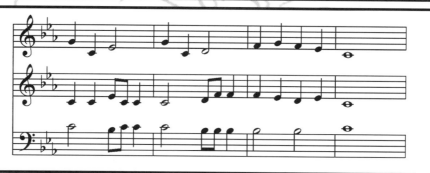

Rhythm for the Road: (Use with the exercises above)

Copyright © 2007, Shawnee Press, Inc., Nashville, TN 37212

Road Trip Four

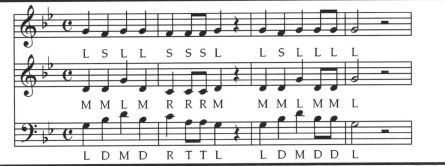

Point of Interest

The last few melodies (starting with Mile 141) have been written in MINOR KEYS. You will notice that they have a different sound and usually end on "La"

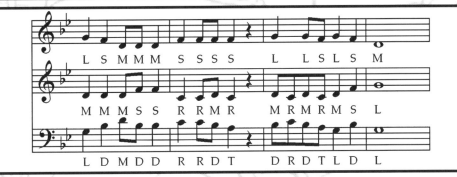

TIME FOR A 150 MILE CHECK-UP!

Rhythm for the Road: (Use with the exercises above)

45

Road Trip Four

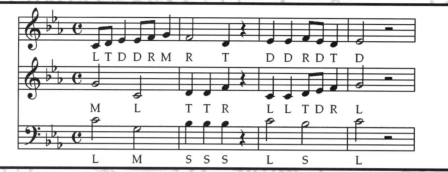

Travel Tip: Try and imagine what our world would be like without music... don't ever take it for granted!

TIME FOR A 155 MILE CHECK-UP!

Rhythm for the Road: (Use with the exercises above)

Copyright © 2007, Shawnee Press, Inc., Nashville, TN 37212

Road Trip Four

Point of Interest

Notice that each measure has only 3 beats on this page. This is called "3/4 Time." It may have a little different feeling than the others.

TIME FOR A 160 MILE CHECK-UP!

Rhythm for the Road: (Use with the exercises above)

Copyright © 2007, Shawnee Press, Inc., Nashville, TN 37212

You Did It!

You have reached the end of our journey! You should be very proud of the fact that you have come a long way...160 miles to be exact.

Please take a moment to go back to Mile 1 and try it...doesn't it seem so easy now? Even though there is much more to learn about reading music, you should now be able to look at a melody and sing it. Just as we said in the beginning, your goal was to train your eyes, ears, and singing voice to work together when reading music.

Please continue to practice reading music...it is a skill you must use regularly if you want to remember how to do it. Also, continue exploring new music every chance you get. Bye for now!